W9-AMP-314

Horses

Shetland
Ponies

by Erin Monahan

Consulting Editor: Gail Saunders-Smith, PhD

Capstone
press

Mankato, Minnesota

Pebble Books are published by Capstone Press,
151 Good Counsel Drive, P.O. Box 669, Mankato, Minnesota 56002.
www.capstonepress.com

1 2 3 4 5 6 14 13 12 11 10 09

Library of Congress Cataloging-in-Publication Data
Monahan, Erin, 1977 –
    Shetland ponies / by Erin Monahan.
    p. cm. — (Pebble books. Horses)
    Includes bibliographical references and index.
    Summary: "A brief introduction to the characteristics, life cycle, and uses of
the Shetland pony breed" — Provided by publisher.
    ISBN-13: 978-1-4296-2235-6 (hardcover)
    ISBN-10: 1-4296-2235-0 (hardcover)
    1. Shetland pony — Juvenile literature. I. Title.
SF315.2.S5M66 2009
636.1'6 — dc22   2008026822

8910

Note to Parents and Teachers

The Horses set supports national science standards related to
life science. This book describes and illustrates Shetland ponies.
The images support early readers in understanding the text. The
repetition of words and phrases helps early readers learn new
words. This book also introduces early readers to subject-specific
vocabulary words, which are defined in the Glossary section. Early
readers may need assistance to read some words and to use the
Table of Contents, Glossary, Read More, Internet Sites, and Index
sections of the book.

Table of Contents

A Child's Pony

The Shetland pony
is gentle but determined.
These ponies are popular
for children to ride.

A pony is smaller
than a horse.
Shetland ponies
stand 42 inches
(107 centimeters) tall.

Shetland ponies have strong legs and hooves. It's easy for them to walk on rocky ground.

Shetland ponies grow
thick coats and manes.
Their coats are
black, bay, or
many other colors.

From Foal to Adult

Female Shetlands give birth to one foal at a time. Foals weigh 15 to 20 pounds (7 to 9 kilograms) at birth.

14

Shetlands learn quickly, but they can be stubborn. They sometimes don't follow directions.

Shetlands are adults
after four years.
They can live for 30 years.

Strong and Gentle

Shetlands are used
for driving.
These strong ponies
can easily pull an adult
in a cart.

Children enjoy riding
and caring for
their Shetland ponies.

Glossary

bay — brown with a black mane and tail

determined — having a firm or fixed purpose

driving — using a harness on a horse so it can pull a cart, wagon, sleigh, or carriage

foal — a young horse or pony

gentle — kind and calm

hoof — the hard covering over the foot of a horse or pony; more than one hoof is hooves.

mane — long, thick hair that grows on the head and neck of some animals such as horses and ponies

popular — liked by many people

stubborn — not willing to give in or change

Read More

Dell, Pamela. *Shetland Ponies.* Majestic Horses. Chanhassen, Minn.: Child's World, 2007.

Pitts, Zachary. *The Pebble First Guide to Horses.* Pebble First Guides. Mankato, Minn.: Capstone Press, 2009.

Internet Sites

FactHound offers a safe, fun way to find educator-approved Internet sites related to this book.

Here's what you do:
1. Visit *www.facthound.com*
2. Choose your grade level.
3. Begin your search.

This book's ID number is 9781429622356.

FactHound will fetch the best sites for you!

23

Index

Word Count: 134

Grade: 1

Early-Intervention Level: 16

Editorial Credits

Erika L. Shores, editor; Bobbi J. Wyss, designer;
Sarah L. Schuette, photo shoot direction

Photo Credits

AP Images/Oneonta Daily Star/Julie Lewis, 18
Capstone Press/Karon Dubke, cover, 1, 6, 10, 12, 14; TJ Thoraldson Digital
Photograhy, 16
Corbis/Kit Houghton, 8
Newscom/Icon S/Action Plus/Martin Cushen, 4
Peter Arnold/Biosphoto/Fruhinsholz Catherine, 20

The Capstone Press Photo Studio thanks Rick Brown and Linda Dinesen for their
help with photo shoots.

Capstone Press thanks Robert Coleman, PhD, associate professor of
Equine Extension at the University of Kentucky, Lexington's Department
of Animal Sciences, for reviewing this book.

2010